Of Atoms and Ocean

Kadee Carder and Amy Cefoldo

Published by Addison Multimedia, 2024.

In Memory of Betty McRight

***

For Granddad Myron and Grandma Connie, who
made sure our family knew Jesus, the importance of
showing up for all the moments, and to never leave the
house without putting on your shoes.

Day 1

PSALM 34:4-5

"I sought the Lord, and He answered me and delivered me from all my fears. Those who look to Him are radiant with joy; their faces will never be ashamed."

"It takes time to extract joy from life" (Elizabethtown). These words were spoken as Orlando Bloom's character dances in a field, waving one hand in the air. He did this only a few short days after his father suddenly passed away from a heart attack and he was fired from his job after losing the company almost a billion dollars.

Joy.

It appears differently to different people, but we all crave it.

Dear Seeker, throughout the next days you will have the opportunity to reflect on life, purpose, joy, and healing. Maybe you need to slow down. Maybe you need to take that daring first step.

Upon each page, you will find an opportunity to choose for that day if you need a Risk or to Reflect. Pick one. Gather a journal or use the pages included to write your thoughts, what you did, felt, or thought along the way.

Breathe.

Feel.

Read those again.

But through all of it, we hope you experience Joy.

Risk: Take a twenty-four-hour break from the internet.

Reflect: What does 'joy' mean to you? How does it differ from happiness, contentment, or peace?

Journal

Journal

Day 2

PSALM 139:13-17

"For it was You who created my inward parts;
You knit me together in my mother's womb.
I will praise You
because I have been remarkably and wonderfully made.
Your works are wonderful,
and I know this very well.
My bones were not hidden from You
when I was made in secret,
when I was formed in the depths of the earth.
Your eyes saw me when I was formless;
all my days were written in Your book and planned
before a single one of them began."

There is no one else like you. There is no one else who has
your fingerprints. In all of time before you arrived on Earth,
and in the time to come, there will never be anyone just like
you. Among the throngs of galaxies, the swirling nebulas, the
whirling arcs of energy and heat in the stars, among the masses
of souls since time began and when it ends, there is only one
you. You are created with unique gifts, abilities, skills, laughter,
art, and thoughts — and you are entrusted with good work

from your Creator. You are designed with purpose. You are millions of atoms amidst an ocean of light. You are loved immeasurably more than you understand.

Risk: Take a picture of yourself that makes you smile.

Reflect: Write a love letter to your body. Include all the ways it helps you experience the world.

Journal

Journal

Day 3

2 CORINTHIANS 2:14-17

"But thanks be to God, who always causes us to triumph in Christ and through us spreads the aroma of the knowledge of Him in every place. For to God we are the fragrance of Christ among those who are being saved and among those who are perishing. To some we are an aroma of death leading to death, but to others, an aroma of life leading to life. And who is competent for this?"

My husband climbed into the car and immediately demanded, "What is that smell?" The two girls in the back seat had just arrived from school, and I stated, "It's probably the been-at-school smell."

He said, "No. I've smelled that before. This is different."

My youngest pointed at her decorated pumpkin in the seat beside her. "Is it my pumpkin?"

She'd bought it herself. Not realizing how heavy it was, she plopped it on a chair in our media room until it could be decorated for the contest. The next day, my husband noticed an orange liquid in the chair. The pumpkin had a crack almost all the way around it. He glued the pumpkin shut so my daughter could decorate it. A week later, with that pumpkin in the car seat, we could smell its demise.

Once we arrived at home, I lit a new pumpkin candle, which freshened up our living room quickly. Sprayed some "I Am Fearless" perfume. Rubbed grapefruit-scented lotion on my hands. Scents stay with us and ignite certain memories, senses, and feelings. What kind of scent are you?

Risk: Find some fresh flowers. Breathe in their scent.

Reflect: What is the best smell in the world? What is the most nostalgic smell for you? Why?

Journal

Journal

Day 4

2 PETER 1:5-8

"Do your best to improve your faith by adding goodness, understanding, self-control, patience, devotion to God, concern for others, and love. If you keep growing in this way, it will show that what you know about our Lord Jesus Christ has made your lives useful and meaningful."

"Time under tension." I first heard this phrase in a workout class where we lift weights choreographed to music. Sometimes the choreography makes us move quickly and then transition into slower movements. The times where we hold in a squat or shift into a deeper range of movement, and then hold, makes the muscles adapt, learn, and grow. Waiting is a training session. It shows you who you are. It shows where you can continue to adapt, learn, and grow. Sometimes that is a hard lesson. However, God made humans fascinating creatures. He allows us to look at who we are, and then build our spiritual physique to be more like Him. Maybe you need to sink lower in that squat. Maybe you need to learn how to wait. Maybe you need to move on to the next set of choreography. What can you do today to make it meaningful?

Risk: Write down three things you want to learn well. Take thirty minutes to work on improving that skill.

Reflect: Describe a memorable dream. Write it down. What do you think it means?

Journal

Journal

Day 5

PSALM 27:1-6
"The Lord is my light and my salvation—
whom should I fear?
The Lord is the stronghold of my life—
of whom should I be afraid?
When evildoers came against me to devour my flesh,
my foes and my enemies stumbled and fell.
Though an army deploys against me,
my heart is not afraid;
though a war breaks out against me,
still I am confident.
I have asked one thing from the Lord;
it is what I desire:
to dwell in the house of the Lord
all the days of my life,
gazing on the beauty of the Lord
and seeking Him in His temple.
For He will conceal me in His shelter
in the day of adversity;
He will hide me under the cover of His tent;
He will set me high on a rock.
Then my head will be high
above my enemies around me;

I will offer sacrifices in His tent with shouts of joy.
I will sing and make music to the Lord."

Throughout our lives, moments of crushing darkness, seemingly unwinnable battles, and incredible loss will find us. But amid the chaos, God promises His light shines brighter than the blackest night. He provides strength for us to grasp, a safe haven from enemies, and an unshakable army fighting our battles. Although we are not guaranteed a life without troubles, God assures us of His constant love and brings us into His tent to take shelter. So, when you feel as though the weight of darkness may overcome you, take heart knowing God's light always wins and even a spark illuminates the deepest shadows.

Risk: Go for a thirty-minute walk. At fifteen minutes along the path, take a moment to yell out a truth about God.

Reflect: What is your definition of love? Write down your definition and how you show love to others. How does God show his love to you?

Journal

Journal

Day 6

1 PETER 5:5B-7

"In the same way, you younger men, be subject to the elders. And all of you clothe yourselves with humility toward one another, because God resists the proud but gives grace to the humble.

Humble yourselves, therefore, under the mighty hand of God, so that He may exalt you at the proper time, casting all your care on Him, because He cares about you."

The definition of the word humility often gets lost in translation. It contains multiple meanings. Essentially, it means, 'to know one's place.' Humility realizes there is always someone 'above' and someone 'below.' It is to recognize status or rank. Just like in the armed forces, there are ranks. Generals, captains, lieutenants, privates, citizens. Each one has a certain job to do and a place to do it; there are people to admire, people to care for, and others for whom to set an example. There is always going to be someone 'better off' and someone 'worse off.' Thinking you don't matter is just as harmful as thinking you are the only one who matters.

These verses remind to 'clothe yourself' with humility. Accept the many layers of your role – you are above others, you are below others; you have certain people under your care, and you are under the care of others. Humility recognizes that you matter. Humility recognizes that each human brings something special to the table.

Risk: Tell someone under your care five things you like about them and then hug them for longer than is comfortable.

Reflect: Write down five things you love about yourself and with whom you would like to share those qualities.

Journal

Journal

Day 7

MATTHEW 26:69-75

"Now, Peter was sitting outside in the courtyard. A servant approached him and she said, 'You were with Jesus the Galilean too.'

But he denied it in front of everyone: 'I don't know what you're talking about!'

When he had gone out to the gateway, another woman saw him and told those who were there, 'This man was with Jesus the Nazarene!'

And again he denied it with an oath, 'I don't know the man!'

After a little while those standing there approached and said to Peter, 'You certainly are one of them, since even your accent gives you away.'

Then he started to curse and to swear with an oath, 'I do not know the man!' Immediately a rooster crowed, and Peter remembered the words Jesus had spoken, 'Before the rooster crows, you will deny Me three times.' And he went outside and wept bitterly."

JOHN 21:15-17

"When they had eaten breakfast, Jesus asked Simon Peter, 'Simon, son of John, do you love Me more than these?'

'Yes, Lord,' he said to Him, 'You know that I love You.'

'Feed My lambs,' He told him. A second time He asked him, 'Simon, son of John, do you love Me?'

'Yes, Lord,' he said to Him, 'You know that I love You.'

'Shepherd My sheep,' He told him. He asked him the third time, 'Simon, son of John, do you love Me?'

Peter was grieved that He asked him the third time, 'Do you love Me?' He said, 'Lord, You know everything! You know that I love You.'

'Feed My sheep,' Jesus said."

Peter ran away when faced with immense pressure. The big moment arrived when he *should have* done the 'right thing,' but he did not. How many times do you think he slapped his palm against his forehead, replaying it in his mind? God intentionally redeemed his story.

Peter was not a lost cause. Neither are you. Peter went on to write many important letters to the church and to shepherd God's sheep. Peter is more than his mistakes. So are you. Your failures help you grow. For each denial and rejection, Jesus restored Peter's heart. It required Peter to jump out of his boat to run to Jesus. He restores hearts. What is your next step today?

Risk: Talk to the oldest person you know and ask for their story.

Reflect: Set a timer for ten minutes. Write down what you consider to be your biggest accomplishment. What have you overcome?

Journal

Journal

Day 8

JAMES 1:19-25

"My dearly loved ones, understand this: Everyone must be quick to hear, slow to speak, and slow to anger, for man's anger does not accomplish God's righteousness. Therefore, ridding yourselves of all moral filth and evil, humbly receive the implanted word, which is able to save you.

But be doers of the word and not hearers only, deceiving yourselves. Because if anyone is a hearer of the word and not a doer, he is like a man looking at his own face in a mirror. For he looks at himself, goes away, and immediately forgets what kind of man he was. But the one who looks intently into the perfect law of freedom and perseveres in it, and is not a forgetful hearer but one who does good works—this person will be blessed in what he does."

People are creatures of habit when it comes to learning something new. They have a pattern. Now, everyone handles 'new' in a unique manner. However, as a fitness instructor and an online teacher, I experience quite a few of these 'this is new' interactions. In fitness, when a new person walks into my class, there are often blank stares, the confused crunching of the forehead wrinkles, and slow or awkward movements.

The new person will often stare at me, absorbing information, and sometimes the person will do the opposite of what I am saying. And that's okay. Beginners need wiggle room to figure out what, how, and why they are doing what they are doing. If there are mirrors available, the class can have the instructor's example in front of them, and their reflections to see how they are doing. With this combination, every consistent member improves. Practice makes progress. Progress requires perseverance. And perseverance is sometimes the entire lesson itself.

Risk: Let someone off the hook for a mistake made.

Reflect: What do you need to forgive yourself for?

Journal

Journal

Day 9

COLOSSIANS 2:4-10

"I am saying this so that no one will deceive you with persuasive arguments. For I may be absent in body, but I am with you in spirit, rejoicing to see how well ordered you are and the strength of your faith in Christ.

Therefore, as you have received Christ Jesus the Lord, walk in Him, rooted and built up in Him and established in the faith, just as you were taught, overflowing with gratitude.

Be careful that no one takes you captive through philosophy and empty deceit based on human tradition, based on the elemental forces of the world, and not based on Christ. For the entire fullness of God's nature dwells bodily in Christ, and you have been filled by Him, who is the head over every ruler and authority."

"Dis-aster is separation from the stars. Such separation is disaster indeed. When we are separated from the stars, the sea, each other, we are in danger of being separated from God" (Madeleine L'Engle, A Stone for a Pillow: Journeys with Jacob). When disaster strikes, falling apart or withdrawing often feels like the right thing, or the easiest, or the default thing, to do. But the real disaster is to withdraw from Christ

Jesus the Lord. He is the filler of space, the great guardian, the man with a plan. Have you felt like you are wandering amidst a disaster? Have you told your best friend about it? To add on – what have you told your Maker about it? He's there in it with you. He's experienced the feelings, too. Can you perhaps draw near to His heart instead of withdrawing? It may be difficult, or feel strange, to accept that your plan may not be the best plan. But sometimes, the plan is so much bigger than we can imagine. And if you go look at the stars, and truly consider how big they are and how far away they are, and how small you are...know that the One who made it all waits right there with you.

Risk: Start a friendly prank war with another family.

Reflect: What distracts you most from being present in your life?

Journal

Journal

Day 10

HEBREWS 13:5-8

"Your life should be free from the love of money. Be satisfied with what you have, for He Himself has said, 'I will never leave you or forsake you.' Therefore, we may boldly say: The Lord is my helper; I will not be afraid. What can man do to me?

Remember your leaders who have spoken God's word to you. As you carefully observe the outcome of their lives, imitate their faith. Jesus Christ is the same yesterday, today, and forever."

The unknown author of Hebrews finishes the letter with a quick checklist of 'to-do' reminders. Most importantly, the author notes that the Lord has declared His constant presence, loyalty, and consistency. Because He is the steadfast friend, He can be trusted and proves trustworthy. More than human money or plans, the Lord has a plan for good. Often, when we become settled in our daily routine, we can forget about how constant and reliable He is, or forget His plan often differs from our limited perspective. When we get outside of our comfort zones, that's the playground where humans thrive. Are you noticing that you don't see far beyond your own two feet?

Or do you think that you can see far down a predictable road? Humans too often think they know where the road goes. But God has an adventure awaiting you. It will contain hills, bumps, muddy roads, and lush valleys. He's there with you along the journey; a constant companion in your choose-your-own-adventure story.

Risk: Go somewhere new.

Reflect: When did you last push the limits of your comfort zone? What did you like about yourself in that zone?

Journal

Journal

Day 11

PSALM 98:1-6

"Sing a new song to the Lord,
for He has performed wonders;
His right hand and holy arm
have won Him victory.
The Lord has made His victory known;
He has revealed His righteousness
in the sight of the nations.
He has remembered His love
and faithfulness to the house of Israel;
all the ends of the earth
have seen our God's victory."
"Shout to the Lord, all the earth;
be jubilant, shout for joy, and sing.
Sing to the Lord with the lyre,
with the lyre and melodious song.
With trumpets and the blast of the ram's horn
shout triumphantly
in the presence of the Lord, our King."

The creative author who crafted, carved, organized, and painted this universe placed His artistry within His creations.

God, the great poet, gave His people a song to sing, music to play, rhythm to rollick, color to coordinate, and words to structure the inner workings of their hearts and minds. He speaks to us through art. And we can speak to Him, and each other, sharing offerings of joy, encouragement, and communication, or of loss, insecurity, and those questions that sometimes cannot be expressed with words. David's psalm encourages listeners to sing a new song. As Matthew Henry's commentary states, "'Sing a most excellent song, the best song you have.' Let the song of Christ's love be like Solomon's on that subject, a song of songs. A song of praise for redeeming love is a new song, such a song as had not been sung before; for this is a mystery which was hidden from ages and generations. Converts sing a new song, very different from what they had sung; they change their wonder and change their joy, and therefore change their note." It's okay if today your art is small and quiet, or if it is loud and big; do it in the presence of the King.

Risk: Get tickets to a live concert or play. Start a standing ovation when you go.

Reflect: Listen to a song that reminds you of a significant memory. Write out the lyrics.

Journal

Journal

Day 12

PSALM 34:18

"The Lord is near the brokenhearted; He saves those crushed in spirit."

Plot structure in a story often relates to real life. Characters face conflict, must make decisions and deal with the consequences of their choices, and then their characterization shifts. Good characters grow and change. Heroes begin as regular protagonists, then face various conflicts to become a hero. Many enter the story as unlikely heroes and must work to become honorable and strong. Some don't want to face conflict, but they must do it anyway. You and I also earn the opportunity to deal with supporting characters and antagonizing events which shape us. Our great Author created storytelling. He invented the concept of conflict shaping characters. He understands that even the strongest of us needs a good supporting side character and some comfort along the way. Think of your favorite protagonist and those characters who stayed or supported along the way. Who are you in your hero story? Who are your supporting characters? Remember that God is our great rescuer, a master storyteller, who knows that you will thrive with opportunities to engage and grow. He will send support, maybe through a family member or friend, but He is also there, by your side on the journey. Maybe you need some support – and maybe you need to be supportive. Often, what you feel you need the most is what you can offer to those around you.

Risk: Send a note of encouragement (to someone you least want to send it to).

Reflect: Write down why you want to let go of your biggest regret. What will happen if you keep holding on to it?

Journal

Journal

Day 13

NEHEMIAH 1:3-4

"They said to me, 'The remnant in the province, who survived the exile, are in great trouble and disgrace. Jerusalem's wall has been broken down, and its gates have been burned down.' When I heard these words, I sat down and wept. I mourned for a number of days, fasting and praying before the God of heaven. I said, 'Yahweh, the God of heaven, the great and awe-inspiring God who keeps His gracious covenant with those who love Him and keep His commands, let Your eyes be open and Your ears be attentive to hear Your servant's prayer that I now pray to You day and night for Your servants, the Israelites. I confess the sins we have committed against You. Both I and my father's house have sinned. We have acted corruptly toward You and have not kept the commands, statutes, and ordinances You gave Your servant Moses. Please remember what You commanded Your servant Moses: 'If you are unfaithful, I will scatter you among the peoples. But if you return to Me and carefully observe My commands, even though your exiles were banished to the ends of the earth, I will gather them from there and bring them to the place where I chose to have My name dwell.' They are Your servants and Your people. You redeemed them by Your great power and strong hand. Please, Lord, let Your ear be attentive to the prayer of Your servant and to that of Your servants who delight to revere Your name. Give Your servant success today, and have compassion on him in the presence of this man."

Nehemiah is known for his work rebuilding Jerusalem. He saw a problem and continued to follow through on a solution, even when it appeared overwhelming. He rebuilt a gigantic wall around the city, one stone at a time. Did it happen all in one day? Did it happen quickly and easily? No, and no. But with prayer, consistent effort, and belief that he was doing the job that God allowed him the opportunity to do, he did it. Good work can be hard work. Hard work can be completed, one stone at a time.

Risk: Make a space more beautiful. For a bigger risk, pick a more public spot.

Reflect: What four words describe your first impression to someone? What four words describe your ideal first impression of others?

Journal

Journal

Day 14

HEBREWS 13:16

"Don't neglect to do what is good and to share, for God is pleased with such sacrifices."

Have you ever been a recipient of a kind act? One time, I received an anonymous envelope full of cash, with a note stating something to the effect of, "I was just thinking about you and thought you could use this. In the past I have been given some extra, so now I pass along that idea to you." Another birthday, my sister-in-law randomly sent me a generous gift. An anonymous couple at my church paid a large sum toward my Master's degree. On other occasions, I have received flowers, goodie baskets, and little trinkets or notes from people who shared with me, "just because." One Thanksgiving, I collected my daughter and we took goodie baskets to some friends' houses, and anonymously dropped them off with a note of encouragement. We laughed so much as we rang the doorbell, ran away to the car, and huddled, breathless, in the front seat, watching from a distance. The definition of "share" is, "a part or portion of a larger amount which is divided among a number of people," or, "to have a portion of (something) with another or others." Seasons come and go where sometimes you can use an extra share, or you can give an extra share. Have you been able to give an extra portion to someone who might need it? Or has someone ever passed along an extra portion to you? It may not be the 'thing' that gets shared, but the fact that someone cared enough to give it, that truly makes a difference.

Risk: Bake cookies and deliver them to a neighbor you haven't met yet.

Reflect: When were you changed by someone else's kindness?

Journal

Journal

Day 15

HEBREWS 10:24-25

"Let us hold on to the confession of our hope without wavering, for He who promised is faithful. And let us consider how we may spur one another on toward love and good deeds, not giving up meeting together, as some are in the habit of doing, but encouraging one another — and all the more as you see the day approaching."

According to the interwebs, forty-three percent of all people who create New Year resolutions expect to fail before February, and almost one out of four quit within the first week. Most people quit before the end of January, and only nine percent see their resolutions through until completion. Why do they quit? Their reasons include lost motivation, being too busy, shifting goals or priorities, or poor timing for setting the resolution. There's always an excuse to give up or quit. Motivation and perseverance engage when they realize the stakes. Sometimes, asking questions helps.

Why stick with faith? What's at stake if you don't?

Why continue meeting with friends (and family)? What is at stake if you do not?

Risk: Confirm a get-together with your besties. Coffee date, dinner date, slumber party?

Reflect: When was the last time you did something for the first time? When was the last time you completed something that felt impossible?

Journal

Journal

Day 16

1 TIMOTHY 1:3-5

"I thank God, whom I serve, as my ancestors did, with a clear conscience, as night and day I constantly remember you in my prayers. Recalling your tears, I long to see you, so that I may be filled with joy. I am reminded of your sincere faith, which first lived in your grandmother Lois and in your mother Eunice and, I am persuaded, now lives in you also."

What's in your closet? Do you have any clothes, coats, blankets, belts, or scarves that have been passed down to you from friends or family? I have a couple of scarves from my grandma, a coat from my grandmother, scarves knitted by my sister, some blankets from my mom, and workout leggings from one of my friends. Do you think you will pass along any pieces that you value? Or do you pass along items that you don't value? I often think about what I want to pass along to those I love, and it is usually based on positive traits, like courage, kindness, and leadership. It's easy to let those negative characteristics like anxiety, bitterness, or fear sit around. But what's different between clothes and intangibles, is that what you use often will last longer. A pair of pants will wear out over time, whereas courage grows stronger and more resilient. Use what you need and watch it shine.

Risk: Organize your closet. Get rid of one item or anything that does not make you feel fabulous.

Reflect: What one item in your closet makes you feel most comfortable? What one word describes how it makes you feel? Why do you need that?

Journal

Journal

Day 17

ISAIAH 45:3-7

"I will give you the treasures of darkness
and riches from secret places,
so that you may know that I, Yahweh,
the God of Israel call you by your name.
I call you by your name,
because of Jacob My servant
and Israel My chosen one.
I give a name to you,
though you do not know Me.
I am Yahweh, and there is no other;
there is no God but Me.
I will strengthen you,
though you do not know Me,
so that all may know from the rising of the sun to its setting
that there is no one but Me.
I am Yahweh, and there is no other.
I form light and create darkness,
I make success and create disaster;
I, Yahweh, do all these things."

I love sunlight. Give me sunshine. Give me summer and sun and warm Texas afternoons, please. However, falling asleep in the calm, cloudy dark of night allows my mind and body to rest much more easily than on a bright, glaring sunny day. The contrast of dark versus light allows us to appreciate each one. If we only had sunny summer days, we surely would grow bored with them. Because the darkness chases the light, we can appreciate both. Often, 'darkness' can be related to scandals or hard times or sadness. These too can be a gift — a gift of experience. How does the air shift when the sun sets? How does the breeze stir upon sunrise? Sometimes the darkness is simply the first step in appreciating the honor of the light.

Risk: Get up early and watch the sun rise, intentionally.

Reflect: What do you look forward to when you wake up in the morning?

Journal

Journal

Day 18

2 CORINTHIANS 6:3-10

"We give no opportunity for stumbling to anyone, so that the ministry will not be blamed. But as God's ministers, we commend ourselves in everything: by great endurance, by afflictions, by hardship, by difficulties, by beatings, by imprisonments, by riots, by labors, by sleepless nights, by times of hunger, by purity, by knowledge, by patience, by kindness, by the Holy Spirit, by sincere love, by the message of truth, by the power of God; through weapons of righteousness on the right hand and the left, through glory and dishonor, through slander and good report; as deceivers yet true; as unknown yet recognized; as dying and look — we live; as being disciplined yet not killed; as grieving yet always rejoicing; as poor yet enriching many; as having nothing yet possessing everything."

2 CORINTHIANS 7:1, 4, 5-7

"...Therefore, dear friends, since we have such promises, let us cleanse ourselves from every impurity of the flesh and spirit, bringing holiness to completion in the fear of God.

I have great confidence in you; I have great pride in you. I am filled with encouragement; I am overcome with joy in all our afflictions.

In fact, when we came into Macedonia, we had no rest. Instead, we were troubled in every way: conflicts on the outside, fears inside. But God, who comforts the humble, comforted us by the arrival of Titus, and not only by his arrival, but also by the comfort he received from you."

Conflict and fear intimidate all people. Let God comfort you. God uses challenges to grow us closer to His heart. Your Creator, Provider, and Shepherd works through your weaknesses to show you HE *is* strong enough. Affliction leads to growth. These verses remind us that the Christian life calls for courageous faith. Courage is the willingness to act in the midst of fear. Be ready with a word of encouragement when conflict or fear begin to strike. Look to God's goodness and what He has done. Do you see Him?

Risk: Read a chapter in a book by candlelight.

Reflect: What do you value the most in a friend? Are you that kind of friend?

Journal

Journal

Day 19

PSALM 145:1-9

"I exalt you, my God the King,
And bless your name forever and ever.
I will bless you every day;
I will praise your name forever and ever.
The LORD is great and is highly praised;
His greatness is unsearchable.
One generation will declare your works to the next
And will proclaim your mighty acts.
I will speak of your splendor and glorious majesty
And your wondrous works.
They will proclaim the power
Of your awe-inspiring acts,
And I will declare your greatness.
They will give a testimony of your great goodness
And will joyfully sing of your righteousness.
The LORD is gracious and compassionate,
Slow to anger and great in faithful love.
The LORD is good to everyone;
His compassion rests on all he has made."

Awe-inspired. When was the last time you felt, 'awed' at something? These verses remind us of the beauty God brought to His creation, and how He acted with grace, splendor, and compassion in building His people on this earth. Take a few moments to slow down today and experience His wondrous works. Soft breezes. Cool water drops. Green leaves. Textured fabrics. Vanilla and cinnamon. Juicy fruit. Crisp vegetables. The purring of a kitten. Stars twinkling. Lively sunshine. The songs of the trees. Laughter. The pulse of a beating heart. Do you see, hear – experience – those gifts? What brings awe to you today?

Risk: Use colors (pencils, crayons, markers, paint) and draw a simple picture.

Reflect: What is your favorite color and what does it symbolize?

Journal

Journal

Day 20

COLOSSIANS 1:3B-6, 9-17

"We always thank God, the Father of our Lord Jesus Christ, when we pray for you, for we have heard of your faith in Christ Jesus and of the love you have for all the saints because of the hope reserved for you in heaven. You have already heard about this hope in the message of truth, the gospel that has come to you. It is bearing fruit and growing all over the world, just as it has among you since the day you heard it and recognized God's grace in the truth.

For this reason also, since the day we heard this, we haven't stopped praying for you. We are asking that you may be filled with the knowledge of His will in all wisdom and spiritual understanding, so that you may walk worthy of the Lord, fully pleasing to Him, bearing fruit in every good work and growing in the knowledge of God. May you be strengthened with all power, according to His glorious might, for all endurance and patience, with joy giving thanks to the Father, who has enabled you to share in the saints' inheritance in the light. He has rescued us from the domain of darkness and transferred us into the kingdom of the Son He loves. We have redemption, the forgiveness of sins, in Him.

He is the image of the invisible God, the firstborn over all creation. For everything was created by Him, in heaven and on earth, the visible and the invisible, whether thrones or dominions or rulers or authorities — all things have been created through Him and for Him. He is before all things, and by Him all things hold together."

Imagine the emotions the church of Colossae felt when reading this letter from Paul. I am sure joy and gratitude swept through them, encouraging them to their very core and spurring them on to keep doing the hard work. When someone recognizes not just the outward work done, but also takes the time to see the heart behind it, hope grows, motivation ignites, and lives change. Paul didn't write to churches and people because he thought he was smarter and more holy, but because he deeply loved them. Think about your closest relationships: How have they spoken into your life? How have you spoken into theirs?

Risk: Go on an adventure with a friend by visiting some new place. Be spontaneous. Bonus points if you walk barefoot outside.

Reflect: Write about your closest relationships. How have they spoken into your life? How have you spoken into theirs? Why do you want to cultivate these strong relationships? What will happen if you do not?

Journal

Journal

Day 21

GENESIS 1:1-13

"In the beginning God created the heavens and the earth.

Now the earth was formless and empty, darkness covered the surface of the watery depths, and the Spirit of God was hovering over the surface of the waters. Then God said, 'Let there be light,' and there was light. God saw that the light was good, and God separated the light from the darkness. God called the light 'day,' and He called the darkness 'night.' Evening came and then morning: the first day.

Then God said, 'Let there be an expanse between the waters, separating water from water.' So God made the expanse and separated the water under the expanse from the water above the expanse. And it was so. God called the expanse 'sky.' Evening came and then morning: the second day.

Then God said, 'Let the water under the sky be gathered into one place, and let the dry land appear.' And it was so. God called the dry land 'earth,' and He called the gathering of the water 'seas.' And God saw that it was good. Then God said, 'Let the earth produce vegetation: seed-bearing plants and fruit trees on the earth bearing fruit with seed in it according to their kinds.' And it was so. The earth produced vegetation: seed-bearing plants according to their kinds and trees bearing fruit with seed in it according to their kinds. And God saw that it was good."

Can we know what 'good' means without God's hand in it? He created the concept of 'good.' He intentionally planned and carefully constructed the various elements, the very oxygen, we breathe. He could have left the void as it were, shapeless and cold. But he chose to create. He chose color, and light, and air, and oceans, and greenery. And He chose to bring you here below. Sounds like He doesn't do anything without meticulous intention. If God knows how many grains of sand lay on each shore, how many feathers will grow on the many sweet birds chirping from their nests, and how many apple trees will thrive from each apple, consider that He sees great purpose within you. He has entrusted good work to you. It may be something small, but sometimes small is awesome. What good will you do today?

Risk: Buy a plant to bring the outside into your home.

Reflect: How do live plants make you feel? Why do plants and water display God's abilities?

Journal

Journal

Day 22

PSALM 90:1-4

"Lord, You have been our refuge
in every generation.
Before the mountains were born,
before You gave birth to the earth and the world,
from eternity to eternity, You are God.
You return mankind to the dust,
saying, 'Return, descendants of Adam.'
For in Your sight a thousand years
are like yesterday that passes by,
like a few hours of the night."

When was the last time you slowed down enough to think about the creation of the universe? Or the vastness that is God and the endless time He holds? Before there were stars in the sky or a sun shining bright, before there was dirt, or water, or mountains – before it all, there was God. Consider all the power and imagination God must possess to create the entire universe – He used it all for you. He built spaces for you to create, learn, and experience joy and rest. He shaped it all, not just for your enjoyment, but that through it all you may come to know Him. From the beginning of time to the end,

God calls His children to Him, to find a safe place to land, to discover His truth, and to experience His love. How can that knowledge shape your day today?

Risk: Spend at least thirty minutes doing something that makes you feel alive.

Reflect: What is something in the vast universe that brings a smile to your face? Spend at least five minutes reflecting on how God had you in mind when He created it.

Journal

Journal

Day 23

2 CORINTHIANS 4:1-9

"Since we have this ministry because we were shown mercy, we do not give up. Instead, we have renounced shameful secret things, not walking in deceit or distorting God's message, but commending ourselves to every person's conscience in God's sight by an open display of the truth. But if our gospel is veiled, it is veiled to those who are perishing. In their case, the god of this age has blinded the minds of the unbelievers so they cannot see the light of the gospel of the glory of Christ, who is the image of God. For we are not proclaiming ourselves but Jesus Christ as Lord, and ourselves as your slaves because of Jesus. For God who said, 'Let light shine out of darkness,' has shone in our hearts to give the light of the knowledge of God's glory in the face of Jesus Christ.

Now we have this treasure in clay jars, so that this extraordinary power may be from God and not from us. We are pressured in every way but not crushed; we are perplexed but not in despair; we are persecuted but not abandoned; we are struck down but not destroyed."

Picture a beautiful ceramic mug sitting on the counter. Now, imagine your cat, whose favorite activity is knocking things to the floor, jumping up onto said counter, and pawing the mug over the edge. Can you imagine the state of the mug? Shattered, most likely, and no matter how much glue you use, it will never be useful again. Raise your hand if you sometimes feel like that mug, teetering on the edge, and no matter what choice you make you will fall and shatter. Although the vessel – our heart, which God created – is essentially like a ceramic mug, He did not form us that way to watch us break. He made us that way so His power will shine through when we do NOT shatter. His strength overcomes our weaknesses when we are NOT crushed. His presence envelopes us so we know we are NOT abandoned. No matter what your outward circumstances may be, no matter how many scars you may have, or wounds that need healing, God will pick you up. He will tend every scrape and then shine His glory through every aspect of your story.

Risk: Spend five minutes focusing on your breathing. Inhale deeply into your abdomen for four slow counts, then exhale deeply for four slow counts. Once you have mastered the deep inhalations and exhalations, add on. With every breath in, claim a truth regarding God; with every breath out; release an untruth.

Reflect: What pressure do you feel right now? Why do you feel this pressure? What will happen if you keep holding on to it?

Journal

Journal

Day 24

ISAIAH 9:6-7

"For a child will be born for us,
a son will be given to us,
and the government will be on His shoulders.
He will be named
Wonderful Counselor, Mighty God,
Eternal Father, Prince of Peace.
The dominion will be vast,
and its prosperity will never end.
He will reign on the throne of David
and over his kingdom,
to establish and sustain it
with justice and righteousness from now on and forever.
The zeal of the Lord of Hosts will accomplish this."

Only one name in all of history has the power to overcome the darkness, dispel fear, heal the wounded, and save mankind. No matter the state of the world, because of the name and man of Jesus, we have hope, peace, joy, and strength. Hope knows Jesus rules over all, and His reign is just. Peace fills our souls, and His joy warms our hearts even when all around us may be in chaos. Strength courses through our bodies to overcome every hurdle the world may toss our way. All this and so much more is possible not simply because Jesus was named Jesus, but because God gave Him the name, then Jesus lived the life, endured the death, and rose again.

Risk: What does your name mean? Explore the internet to discover the attributes spoken over you via your given name.

Reflect: How do you see your name's qualities in your life? In what ways are you living as a child of the King?

Journal

Journal

Day 25

HABAKKUK 3:17-19

"Though the fig tree does not bud and there is no fruit on the vines, though the olive crop fails and the fields produce no food, though there are no sheep in the pen and no cattle in the stalls, yet I will triumph in Yahweh; I will rejoice in the God of my salvation! Yahweh my Lord is my strength; He makes my feet like those of a deer and enables me to walk on mountain heights!"

God did not promise a life without trial, but instead a rainbow after every storm, a yoke that is easy if we lay our burdens down, and joy in the morning. When the fridge holds little food and there is no money to fill it; when you lose your job or the car breaks down for the tenth time, or you hear about someone else's dreams coming true – again, it is hard to look to the goodness of God. But what if, even for one day, no matter what circumstances lay in your path, you decide to rejoice in the hardship? Instead of focusing on the lack of whatever it may be, seek out the abundance. Think of trials as, "get to," not "have to." Remember that every hard mountain climb always ends with an amazing view.

Risk: Create a soundtrack for a poignant memory. Include a broad variety of music genres – instrumental, or remixes of your favorites, etc. Listen to it.

Reflect: Commit to not complaining about anything for twenty-four hours. Take notes throughout the day as to how this influences your perspective.

Journal

Journal

Day 26

MATTHEW 5:14-16

"You are the light of the world. A city situated on a hill cannot be hidden. No one lights a lamp and puts it under a basket, but rather on a lampstand, and it gives light for all who are in the house. In the same way, let your light shine before men, so that they may see your good works and give glory to your Father in heaven."

What does it mean to let your light shine for the world to see? Of course, part is sharing God's love with those around you, but also stepping into the work God created you to do. We each have a specific purpose and passion that drives our lives, the decisions we make, and the roads on which we travel. The amazing part is God placed those passions and dreams in our hearts so that His light will shine for the world to see. Every step we take may not bring excitement or even joy, especially in the midst of the basic day-to-day activities and chores, but do not lose hope. It is during the mundane that God builds patience, endurance, empathy, strength, peace, and the list goes on. Your purpose is not a destination, but a journey, one filled with excitement and hard work. In the end, no matter what we may do, God's main desire is for us to simply obey His voice, trust He will provide all we need to know along the way, and remember He never gives up on us. And when we step out in obedience, you better believe He is in the stands cheering us on, beaming wide as He watches His light shine.

Risk: Tap into your creative self. Have you wanted to learn to draw, use oil paints, throw a pottery bowl, write poetry, take a cooking class, rearrange your living room, or sing before an audience, but always held back? Take the first step to accomplishing this.

Reflect: What is something blossoming in you right now? What is holding you back?

Journal

Journal

Day 27

JAMES 1:2-6

"Consider it pure joy, my brothers and sisters, whenever you face trials of many kinds, because you know that the testing of your faith produces perseverance. Let perseverance finish its work so that you may be mature and complete, not lacking anything. If any of you lacks wisdom, you should ask God, who gives generously to all without finding fault, and it will be given to you. But when you ask, you must believe and not doubt, because the one who doubts is like a wave of the sea, blown and tossed by the wind."

How many times, in the middle of something hard, have you stopped and rejoiced for the situation in which you find yourself? I know the first thought that comes to my mind most likely will not be joy, and in some situations, I may struggle to find joy amid the trial. However, James instructs us to rejoice. He instructs this not simply because it is "right," but because focusing on joy and blessing shifts our perspective. It does not take the pain of grief away, or suddenly change the circumstances. It reminds us of God's abundance. When you can pull out little bits of good throughout your day, they begin to stack up. Before you know it, the list of joys is a lot longer than the list of trials. So no matter where you are, no matter what life throws at you, remember that each moment God is building perseverance within you, not just to get through each day, but to conquer whatever comes your way.

Risk: Spend the day making two lists: one list of things big or small that bring you joy, and one list of things that were hard or annoying. At the end of the day, tape your 'joy list' to your bathroom mirror and destroy the other.

Reflect: When was the last time you laughed until you cried? What can you do to bring more laughter into your life?

Journal

Journal

Day 28

PSALM 34:14

"Turn away from evil and do what is good; seek peace and pursue it."

Humans are naturally drawn to conflict. We love stories. Stories are conflict. So this concept of turning away from evil, the concept of pursuing peace, may appear at first to be somewhat of a 'boring' guideline. Where's the adventure in seeking peace? Just like in the game of 'hide and seek,' peace itself is not some waif-like wad of whimsy. Peace requires wisdom, and audacity, and moxie. Peace requires people with a big-picture mindset. Peace is not just a comfortable and happy feeling. The definition is two-fold: first, a freedom from disturbance, or tranquility, and second, a state in which there is no war or war has ended. God has won the war between good and evil; with Jesus' great sacrifice, we have been restored to Him and He has overcome. The End has been written. However, the battles around us continue because we are still in the middle of the adventure. But, we know as fact, the war has been won. Remembering that fact can often be the challenge. Do you surround yourself with those who draw near to the

King of Kings? How can you expand your perimeter of peace today?

Risk: Widen your circle. Start a conversation with a stranger that would ordinarily make you uncomfortable.

Reflect: What person made the biggest impact on who you are right now? What attribute does that person have that you would like to cultivate?

Journal

Journal

Day 29

1 TIMOTHY 1:7

"For God has not given us a spirit of fear, but a spirit of power, love, and a sound mind."

Fear. One little word, yet it encompasses a myriad of things and can bring the strongest to her knees. Fear can feel as if the entire body, mind, and heart are being consumed. The brain malfunctions and starts believing lies, the heart pounds faster and faster, all while the body stands frozen. But we need to remember fear is merely a spirit, and with God's power, you have the strength to expel that spirit. God sends the spirit of power and moves your body. He gives the spirit of love and brings your heartbeat steady with His. God fills you with His sound mind and rewires your brain to think like Him. So, when you face fear, because you will, know that you have every weapon available to not only fight, but come out victorious.

Risk: Sit in the dark alone or in a crowded place, for thirty minutes. Do whichever makes you feel most uncomfortable.

Reflect: What do you need to give yourself permission to feel? What hurts are waiting to be seen? Can God help you either embrace them or let them go?

Journal

Journal

Day 30

PSALMS 90:12, 14, 16, 17

"Teach us to number our days carefully so that we may develop wisdom in our hearts... Satisfy us in the morning with Your faithful love so that we may shout with joy and be glad all our days... Let Your work be seen by Your servants, and Your splendor by their children. Let the favor of the Lord our God be on us; establish for us the work of our hands — establish the work of our hands!

Whether you enjoy mornings or loathe them, you must admit there is something special about those moments right before the sun rises, or before your family or roommates stir, or even that glorious first cup of coffee. No matter what time the clock reads, God desires to experience those kinds of moments with you all day. God is in the sunrise, the quiet mornings, the busy afternoons, the two o'clock coffee, the sunset, the crazy family bedtime routines, and the peaceful nights. He wants your whole day. And when you give Him space in it, those around you can't help but take note. When you allow Him in, joy seeps into your work and pours into everyone around you. Be the one who seeks God in the morning, at work, in the grocery store, stuck in traffic, making dinner, or whatever your day holds. In the end, you will never regret it.

Risk: Dance in the grocery store. Partner up with someone nearby.

Reflect: What are two things you hope others (friends, kids, siblings, co-workers, etc.) will talk about when they describe their memories of you?

Journal

Journal

Day 31

JAMES 1:17-18

"Every good and perfect gift is from above, coming down from the Father of the heavenly lights, who does not change like shifting shadows."

The Milky Way galaxy is made up of at least 100 billion stars. On a clear night, the unaided eye may be able to see between 2,600 and 4,500 brilliant white lights from Earth's surface. On a cloudy night, or a bright moon-filled night, those numbers shift. Have you ever noticed how nighttime has a certain feel to it? There's a calm. There's a slowing down. A cooling. Throughout the day, busy bugs bustle, tires crush through gravel, dogs bark, and humans hustle. And then with twilight, the lights shift into a dark hybrid of calm, vapor, and wings tucked away. As Earth twirls in space, sometimes that lonely feeling can become overwhelming. Where there was activity and checklists, now there's a silence that may feel harsh, and the passing of time often rustles through the nearby grasses. What is night to you?

Nighttime is a gift. Rest, recovery, a necessity. Those precious gifts we don't always notice...the warmth of a fresh cup of coffee in the morning, or a snuggly hug, or a soft blanket, or the songs of the trees overhead. Have you noticed any precious gifts nestled near your fingertips? Every good and perfect gift is from the Father of heavenly lights. He made so many beautiful stars that we cannot count them all. We certainly cannot see them all. Consider all that you do not see, and that although you may not see it now, you may see it soon. Are you looking for it?

Risk: Go outside at night and count one hundred stars.

Reflect: What is one of your favorite things that has happened in the dark?

Journal

Journal

Day 32

PROVERBS 31:15-17, 24-27, 30-31
    "She rises while it is still night
    and provides food for her household
    and portions for her female servants.
    She evaluates a field and buys it;
    she plants a vineyard with her earnings.
    She draws on her strength
    and reveals that her arms are strong.
    She makes and sells linen garments;
    she delivers belts to the merchants.
    Strength and honor are her clothing,
    and she can laugh at the time to come.
    She opens her mouth with wisdom
    and loving instruction is on her tongue.
    She watches over the activities of her household
    and is never idle.
    Charm is deceptive and beauty is fleeting,
    but a woman who honors the Lord will be praised.
    Give her the reward of her labor,
    and let her works praise her at the city gates."

Raise your hand if at any point in your life you read about the Proverbs 31 woman and felt 'less than.' She seems to do it all perfectly, with a loving and praise-filled spirit nonetheless. Who can compete or live up to that? But the truth is the enemy wants us to compare our lives to one another, to believe that if we don't have it all together, we fall short of the 'ideal woman.' God, however, says, "She who honors Him will be praised," not, "she who keeps the cleanest house," or "is always patient." God does not expect perfection, only that we seek Him in all we do. He desires one who loves Him even in the midst of the mundane, the hardship, the joy, the trials and triumphs, and do it all with Him by her side.

Risk: Cook a new recipe. Eat it and enjoy the fruit of your labor.

Reflect: What place inspired your favorite recipe? Why do you enjoy that place and that recipe?

Journal

Journal

Day 33

JOB 37:5-7

"God thunders marvelously with His voice; He does great things that we cannot comprehend. For He says to the snow, 'Fall to the earth,' and the torrential rains, His mighty torrential rains, serve as His sign to all mankind, so that all men may know His work."

Sometimes God works obviously. He sends mighty thunderstorms, fantastic lightning shows, answers our prayers exactly how we hoped He would, paints flowers with brilliant colors, provides friendships, laughter, and delicious food to nourish our bodies. Sometimes, God works differently than we think He ought.

A children's cartoon of a cute dog family told the story with the theme, "It will work out like it should," with the iteration of, "We'll see." Throughout the episode, the members of the family tried not to focus on the fact that they were moving. Meanwhile, the family searched for a runaway bride, stopping at a tea shop, finding a coin, and advancing to a local lookout, where the children inserted the coin in a viewfinder machine incorrectly.

The coin stuck. They couldn't see out the viewfinder and were so sad. However, they finally found the bride, went back to their home which was for sale, and enjoyed the fun wedding.

Unknown to them, a couple, who had purchased the dog family's house, stopped at that lookout, used the coin to see the area, and spotted a house with a pool (which they really wanted). So the couple stopped the purchase of the home and bought the house with the pool. The dog family decided to stay in their home and everyone celebrated.

Every part of this little 'random' journey mattered, even though the characters did not realize it at the time. The key step in this process was the lost coin and the viewfinder. While the family members focused on the task at hand, along the journey, small errors and mis-steps created much larger waves than they realized. The family planned on celebrating a wedding day; in the end, a lost coin changed the trajectory of their lives. Sometimes a loss is a gain, but we don't see it. That's where trust comes in. "We will see."

God loves you. God has a plan for good. Sometimes, He has a plan to move, and sometimes a plan to stay. He can use that lost coin. He creates beauty from our miscalculations. Either way, He's on the adventure with you. Look for his craftsmanship today; ask Him to show you how to be brave today.

Risk: Let your skin touch atoms that have been coursing over the earth since the beginning of time. Jump into some water: swim, jump in a puddle, dance in the rain or a sprinkler, bathe.

Reflect: In what ways do you feel out of control in your life?

Journal

Journal

Day 34

ZEPHANIAH 3:14-17
    "Sing, O Daughter of Zion;
    Shout aloud, O Israel!
    Be glad and rejoice with all your heart,
    O Daughter of Jerusalem!
    The Lord has taken away your punishment,
    He has turned back your enemy,
    The Lord, the King of Israel, is with you;
    never again will you fear any harm.
    On that day they will say to Jerusalem,
    "Do not fear, O Zion;
    do not let your hands hang limp.
    The Lord your God is with you,
    He is mighty to save.
    He will take great delight in you,
    He will quiet you with his love,
    He will rejoice over you with singing."

Picture the cutest little girl, dancing and twirling for an audience of one — her daddy. The wide smile on his face, the twinkle in his eye, the loud applause he claps over her performance — all that adoration and love is for her heart and passion. He didn't notice her tripping or missing the beat; all he sees is the daughter he adores. You, my friend, are that child, and God is that father. He sees you, He delights in you, and He pours out His love over you. He forgives any mistakes. He reworks your journey to use past scars for His good. And He proclaims His never-ending joy into the very fabric of your life.

Risk: Encourage someone by either literally applauding or vocally applauding a job he or she performed.

Reflect: What is the "dance" you are performing for God in this era of your life? Take a couple of minutes to bask in God's adoration.

Journal

Journal

Day 35

MATTHEW 14:22-31

"Immediately Jesus made the disciples get into the boat and go ahead of Him to the other side, while He dismissed the crowds. After dismissing the crowds, He went up on the mountain by Himself to pray. When evening came, He was there alone. But the boat was already over a mile from land, battered by the waves, because the wind was against them. Around three in the morning, He came toward them walking on the sea.

When the disciples saw Him walking on the sea, they were terrified. 'It's a ghost!' they said, and cried out in fear.

Immediately Jesus spoke to them. 'Have courage! It is I. Don't be afraid.'

'Lord, if it's You,' Peter answered Him, 'command me to come to You on the water.'

'Come!' He said.

And climbing out of the boat, Peter started walking on the water and came toward Jesus. But when he saw the strength of the wind, he was afraid. And beginning to sink he cried out, 'Lord, save me!'

Immediately Jesus reached out His hand, caught hold of him, and said to him, 'You of little faith, why did you doubt?' When they got into the boat, the wind ceased. Then those in the boat worshiped Him and said, 'Truly You are the Son of God!'"

Courage. It is the ability to do something that frightens; it is also defined as strength in the face of pain or grief. Courage requires action. Sometimes through one small action at a time, courage wills the wanderer to lean into the adventure. Today, Jesus holds out His hand to you, open palms, calling out, "Come!"

He *will* catch you.

"Life moves pretty fast. If you don't stop and look around once in a while, you could miss it" (Ferris Bueller/John Hughes). Perhaps you need to stop and experience the beauty surrounding you. Perhaps you need a gentle reminder to get up and get going. Either way, have courage, just like Jesus commanded.

"Have" means to possess, to own, to experience, or undergo. Own it. Experience strength today, provided by your Creator, who walks on water by your side. Step onward to discover what may arise. It's a rather grand adventure.

Risk: When have you walked on water? Write it down and put the reminder where you see it often.

Reflect: What distractions keep you waiting on the sidelines? What first step can you take to walk closer to Jesus right now?

Journal

Journal

A Special Thank You

IN 2017, THE COMPANY The MomCo, previously known as Mothers of Preschoolers (MOPS) sent out literature with thoughtful questions to its members. These questions and action points were to give each group a twenty-eight-day bonding time so that members could take a moment daily to experience life fully. After receiving permission from MOPS to use some of these questions and actions, we decided to expand those ideas and create a Risk/Reflection time in this devotional. This devotional can be a personal one, but it is also suitable for a family or group to experience together. Sometimes the best adventures include a group of friends or your family.

Our hope is that this thirty-five-day devotional will allow you to experience the textures of life and reflect on the goodness God has gifted you, whether in big or small things.

And if you are a mom, whether of big or little people, go find a local MomCo group to join, because it will change your life forever, for good.

About the Authors
Kadee Carder

FIERCE YET SPARKLY, I rally seekers to thrive in their stories. The goal is magic, the medium is ink, and the fuel is coffee. And sometimes pizza. I teach English on the university level when I'm not dancing around the living room with my family, lifting heavy at the gym, or traveling the planet.

The ALLIANCE series (INSURRECTION, INCOMPLETE, INDELIBLE, HERE BE DRAGONS, EARTHSHINE) and non-fiction inspirational KINGDOM COME and IGNITE roll out perilous motives, twisty plots, and daring protagonists. The ultimate goal for all of my writing is to refresh spirits, point people toward a loving God, and show readers a life thriving. May my stories bring a swift breeze on a stale day, a glow of rejuvenation for your plotline, and a sturdy clap on the back to encourage you on your way.

About the Authors
Amy Cefoldo

THERE ONCE WAS A GIRL, who always had her nose buried in a book, ink staining her hands from scribbling down stories and lost to daydreams of finding her "Happily Ever After." Fast forward a few years (give or take a couple decades) and that girl is still me...with a few minor changes. My nose, of course, will always be found in a book—or five—and I have an ever-growing pile of books to read. I traded in my pen for the clickity-clack of a keyboard and I fill the night creating new worlds. The daydreaming of my "Happily Ever After" came true when I married my nerdy prince and we live in our yellow "castle" with our royal subjects: two adventurous boys and three feisty cats.

"Of Atoms and Oceans" is my debut publication.

Journal

Journal

Journal

Journal

Journal

Journal

Journal

Journal

Journal

Journal

Journal

Journal

Journal

Journal

Journal

Journal

Journal

Journal

Journal

Journal

Also by Kadee Carder

Alliance
Insurrection
Incomplete
Indelible
Here Be Dragons
Earthshine
A Shadow of Jaguars

Standalone
Of Atoms and Ocean

Watch for more at https://www.kadeecarder.com/.

Also by Amy Cefoldo

Of Atoms and Ocean